THE TUPAC SHAKUR COLLECTION

MW00737961

Creative Consultant: Afeni Shakur
Project Manager: Jeannette DeLisa
Book Art Layout: Carmen Fortunato

CONTENTS

R U Still Down?

Written by TUPAC SHAKUR,
JONATHAN BUCK and JOHNNY JACKSON

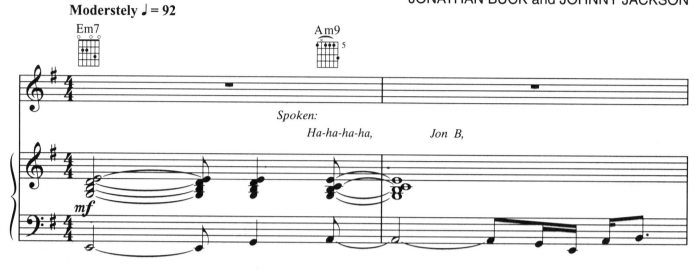

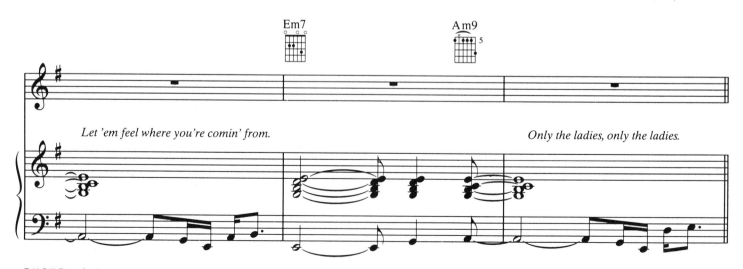

R U Still Down? - 7 - 1
PFM0106

Chorus:
Em7
Am9
Girl, it's al - right,
ba - by,
Are you still down for me now?
Em7
Am9
'cause it's there in your eyes,
yeah.
Are you still down for me now?
Em7
Am9
I can see that you want
me
Are you still down for me now?
Em7
Am9
by the way that you smile.
Yeah, are you still down for me?

6

Verse:

1. Left once a - gain_____ at home,_____
2. *See additional lyrics*

an - oth - er night you're a - lone._____

Ain't no fun in love if you're lov - in' a - lone.___ How does it feel to be

use - less, a - lone?_____ *Tell it.*

Verse 2:
Remember that evening?
(Yeah, baby, are you still down?)
I know that you were too scared to go all the way.
(Please?)
But you did it to please me.
Crying, it was raining when you gave it to me.
The more I see you the more I feel inside.
And I know one day you'll make it back to where you can fly.
(Watch the time go.)
Don't cry.
(Whatcha cryin' for?)
Tomorrow is better days.
Let me dry your eyes, think you're burnin' away.
(To Rap:)

Rap 2:
Only once in a lifetime, touch my soul.
Go slow, Baby Boo, don't rush the flow.
Got me all weak, baby, but I'm strong apart.
With more bounce to the ounce with the longest parts.
Get me mined like fine wine measured in time.
Maybe the other brothers loved you, but the pleasure was mine.
Mama taught me how to love a woman, Papa was sprung.
We committed, so I hit it and it's properly done.
(To Chorus:)

Brenda's Got A Baby

Written by TUPAC SHAKUR
and DEON EVANS

12

Bridge:

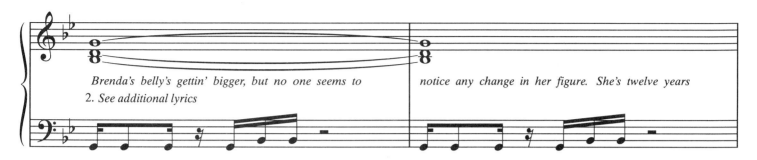

Brenda's belly's gettin' bigger, but no one seems to
2. See additional lyrics

notice any change in her figure. She's twelve years

F

old and she's havin' a baby,   in love with the mo-

lester, who sexed and crazy. And yet and all she

E♭

thinks that he'll be with her forever and dreams of a

world with the two of them are together, whatever. He

1.   *D.S.* 𝄋

F

left her and she had the baby solo. She had it on the

bathroom floor and didn't know so.   3. She didn't know

Repeat ad lib. and fade

don't___ you know___ she's got a ba - by._____

Verse 2:
But oh, that's a thought, my own revelation.
Do whatever it takes ta resist the temptation.
Brenda got herself a boyfriend.
Her boyfriend was her cousin. Now let's watch the joy end.
She tried to hide her pregnancy from her family,
Who really didn't care to see or give a damn if she
Went out and had a church of kids.
As long as when the check came in, they got first dibs.
(To Bridge:)

Verse 3:
She didn't know what ta throw away and what to keep.
She wrapped the baby up and threw him in the trash heap.
I guess she thought she'd get away, wouldn't hear the cries.
She didn't realize how much tha little baby had her eyes.
Now tha baby's in the trash heap, ballin'.
Momma can't help her, but it hurts ta hear her calling.
Brenda wants to run away. Momma say,
"You makin' me lose pay, the social worker's here everyday."
(To Bridge:)

Bridge 2:
Now Brenda's gotta make her own way.
Can't go to her family, they won't let her stay.
No money, no babysitter, she couldn't keep a job.
She tried to sell crack, but end up getting robbed.
So now, what's next? There ain't nothin' left to sell,
So she sees sex as a way of leavin' hell.
It's payin' the rent, so she really can't complain.
Prostitute found slain, and Brenda's her name.
She's got a baby.
(To Ending:)

California Love

Written by TUPAC SHAKUR, ANDRE YOUNG,
ROGER TROUTMAN, LARRY TROUTMAN, MIKEL HOOKS,
RONNIE HUDSON, NORMAN DURHAM and WOODY CUNNINGHAM

Shake it, Cal - i.   Shake it, shake it, ba - by.

Shake it, shake it.   Shake it, shake it, ma - ma.

1.   F 5
2.   F 5

Shake it, Cal - i.   Shake it, Cal - i.

Out on bail,

Ending Rap Section:

G 5   F 5   G 5   F 5

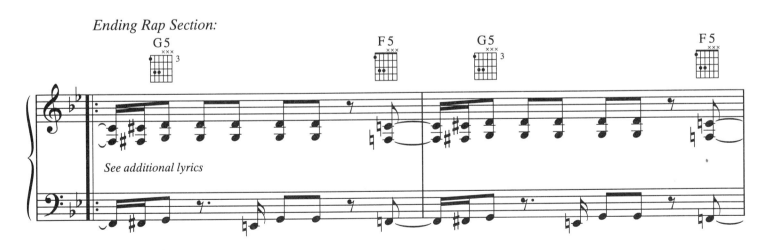

See additional lyrics

Repeat ad lib. and fade

Verse 2:
Out on bail, fresh outta jail, California dreamin'.
Soon as I stepped on the scene, I'm hearin' hootchies screamin'.
Fiendin' for money and alcohol,
The life of a West Side playa where cowards die, and it's all a ball.
Only in Cali, where we riot, not rally to live and die in L.A.
We wearin' Chucks, not Ballies. (That's right.)
Dressed in Locs and Khaki suits and ride is what we do.
Flossin' but have caution, we collide with other crews.
Famous 'cause we program world-wide.
Let 'em recognize from Long Beach to Rosecrans.
Bumpin' and grindin' like a slow jam, it's West Side.
So you know the row won't bow down to no man.
Say what you say, but give me that bomb beat from Dre.
Let me serenade the streets of L.A.
From Oakland to Sacktown, the Bay Area and back down.
Cali is where they put they Mack down.
Give me love.
(To Chorus:)

Ending Rap Section:
Uh, yeah, uh, Long Beach in tha house, uh, yeah.
Oaktown, Oakland definitely in tha house, ha-ha-ha-ha.
Frisco, Frisco.
Hey, you know L.A. up in this.
Pasadena, where you at?
Yeah, Ingelwood, Ingelwood always up to no good.
Even Hollywood tryin' to get a piece, baby.
Sacramento, Sacramento, where ya at? Yeah.
Throw it up, y'all, throw it up, throw it up.
I can't see ya.
California love.

Do For Love

Written by TUPAC SHAKUR,
BOBBY CALDWELL, KENNETH KARLIN,
CARSTEN SCHACK and ALFONS KETTNER

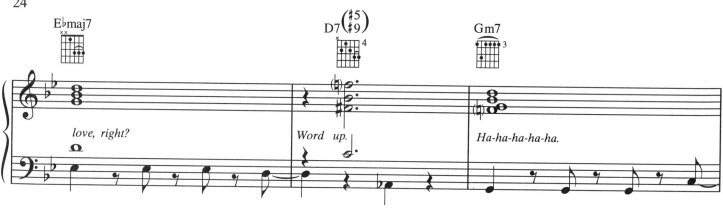

Verse 2:
Just when I thought I broke away and I'm feelin' happy,
You try to trap me, say you pregnant and guess who the daddy.
Don't wanna fall for it, but in this case, what could I do?
So now I'm back to makin' promises to you, tryin' to keep it true.
What if I'm wrong? A trick to keep me on and on.
Tryin' to be strong and in the process, keep you goin'.
I'm 'bout to lose my composure, I'm gettin' close
To packin' up and leavin' notes and gettin' ghost.
Tell me who knows a peaceful place where I can go
To clear my head. I'm feelin' low, losin' control.
My heart is sayin', "Leave." Oh, what a tangled web we weave
When we conspire to deceive. And now you gettin'
Calls at the house, guess you cheatin'.
That's all I need to hear 'cause I'm leavin'. I'm out the do'.
Never no more will you see me. This is the end,
'Cause now I know you've been cheatin'.
I'm a sucka for love.
(To Chorus:)

Verse 3:
Now he left you with scars, tears on your pillow and you still stay.
As you sit and pray, hoping the beatings'll go away.
It wasn't always a hit and run relationship.
It used to be love, happiness and companionship.
Remember when I treated you good?
I moved you up to the hills, out the ills of the ghetto hood.
Me and you a happy home, when it was on.
I had a love to call my own.
I shoulda seen you was trouble, but I was lost, trapped in your eyes.
Preoccupied with gettin' tossed, no need to lie.
You had a man and I knew it. You told me,
"Don't worry 'bout it, we can do it now." I'm under pressure.
Make a decesion 'cause I'm waitin'. When I'm alone,
I'm on the phone havin' secret conversations, huh.
I wanna take your misery, replace it with happiness.
But I need your faith in me. I'm a sucka for love.
(To Chorus:)

Changes

Written by
TUPAC SHAKUR, BRUCE HORNSBY
and DEON EVANS

Verse 2:
I see no changes, all I see is racist faces.
Misplaced hate makes disgrace to races.
We under, I wonder what it takes to make this
One better place, let's erase the wasted.
Take the evil out the people, they'll be acting right,
'Cause both black and white is smokin' crack tonight.
And only time will chill is when we kill each other.
It takes skill to be real, time to heal each other.
And although it seems Heaven sent,
We ain't ready to see a black president, uh.
It ain't a secret, don't conceal the fact
The penitentiary's packed, and it's filled with blacks.
But some things will never change.
Try to show another way, but you stayin' in the dope game.
Now tell me, what's a mother to do?
Bein' real don't appeal to the brother in you.
You gotta operate the easy way.
"I made a G today", but you made it in a sleazy way,
Sellin' crack to the kid. "I gotta get paid."
Well hey, that's the way it is.
(To Chorus:)

Verse 3:
And still I see no changes.
Can't a brother get a little peace.
It's war on the streets and the war in the Middle East.
Instead of war on poverty, they got a war on drugs
So the police can bother me.
And I ain't never did a crime I ain't have to do.
But now I'm back with the blacks givin' it back to you.
Don't let 'em jack you up, back you up,
Crack you up and pimp slap you up.
You gotta learn to hold ya own.
They get jealous when they see ya with a mobile phone.
But tell the cops they can't touch this.
I don't trust this, when they try to rush, I bust this.
That's the sound of my tool, you say it ain't cool.
My mama didn't raise no fool.
And as long as I stay black, I gotta stay strapped
And I never get to lay back.
'Cause I always got to worry 'bout the pay backs,
Some buck that I roughed up way back,
Comin' back after all these years..
Rat-a-tat-tat-tat-tat. That's the way it is, uh.
(To Chorus:)

Dear Mama

Written by
TUPAC SHAKUR, JOE SAMPLE,
TONY PIZARRO, JOSEPH B. JEFFERSON,
CHARLES SIMMONS and BRUCE HAWES

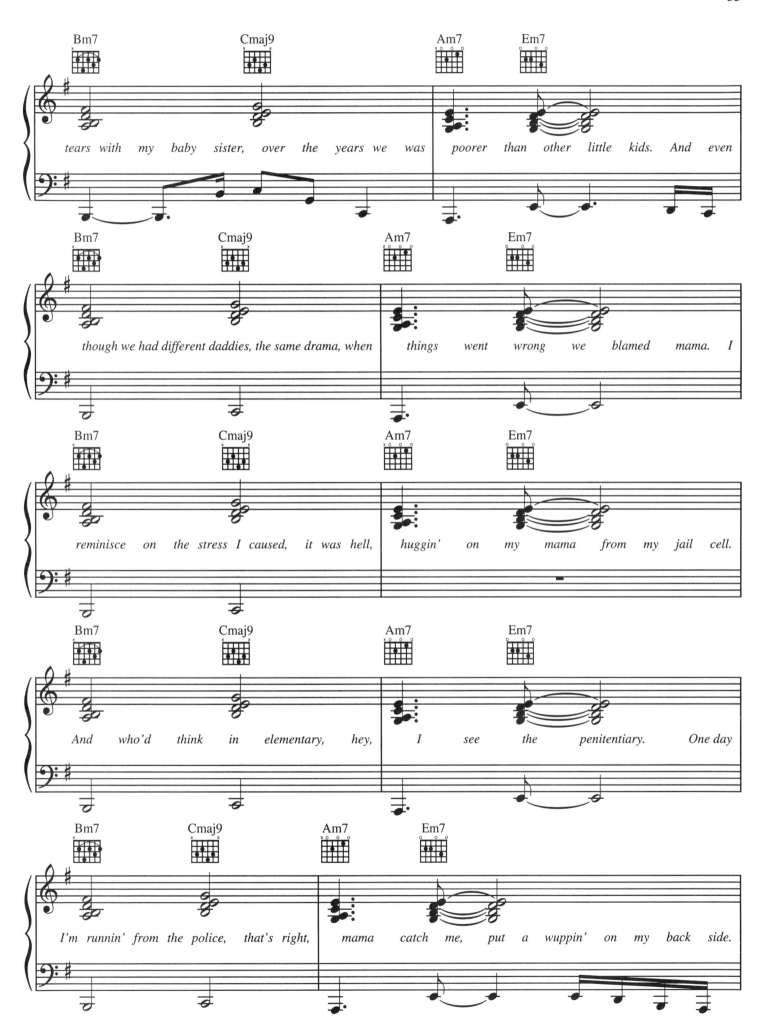

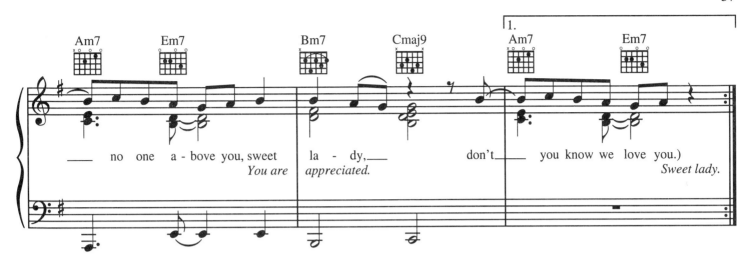

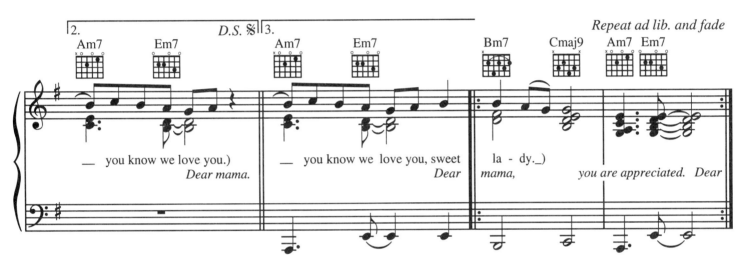

Verse 2:
There ain't nobody tell us it was fair,
No love from daddy 'cause the coward wasn't there.
He passed away and I didn't cry
'Cause my anger wouldn't let me feel for a stranger.
They say I'm wrong and I'm heartless
But all along I was lookin' for a father, he was gone.
I hung around with the thugs,
And even though they sold drugs
They showed a young brother love.
I moved out, started really hangin',
I needed money of my own, so I started slangin'.
I ain't guilty, 'cause even though I sell rocks
It feels good puttin' money in your mail box.
I love payin' rent when the rent's due.
I hope you got the diamond necklace that I sent to you
'Cause when I was low, you was there for me.
You never left me alone because you cared for me
And I could see you comin' home after work late.
In the kitchen tryin' to fix us a hot plate,
Just workin' with the scraps you was given.
And mama made miracles every Thanksgiving
But now the road got rough, you're alone
Tryin' to raise two bad kids on your own.
And there's no way I can pay you back
But my plan is to show you that I understand.
(To Chorus:)

Verse 3:
Pour out some liquor, again I reminisce
'Cause through the drama
I can always depend on my mama.
And when it seems that I'm hopeless
You say the words that can get me back in focus.
When I was sick as a little kid,
To keep me happy, there's no limit to the things you did.
And all my childhood memories,
Full of all the sweet things you did for me.
And even though I act crazy
I gotta thank the Lord that you made me,
There are no words that can express how I feel.
You never kept a secret, always stayed real
And I appreciate how you raised me
And all the extra love that you gave me.
I wish that I could take the pain away
If you can make it through the night
There's a brighter day.
Everything will be alright if you hold on,
It's a struggle everyday, gotta roll on.
There's no way I can pay you back
But my plan is to show you that I understand.
You are appreciated.
(To Chorus:)

How Do U Want It

Written by TUPAC SHAKUR, QUINCY JONES,
LEON WARE, STANLEY RICHARDSON, BRUCE FISHER
and JOHNNY JACKSON

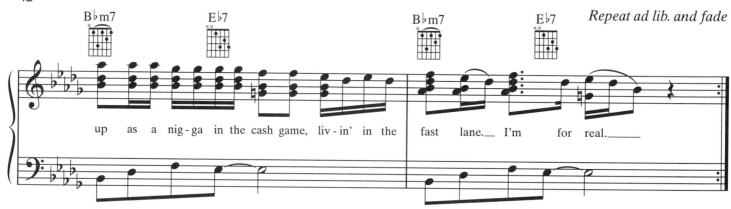

Repeat ad lib. and fade

up as a nig-ga in the cash game, liv-in' in the fast lane.__ I'm for real._____

Verse 2:
Tell me, is it cool to fuck?
Did you think I come to talk, am I a fool, or what?
Positions on the floor, it's like erotic, ironic,
'Cause I'm somewhat psychotic.
I'm hittin' switches on bitches like I been fixed with hydraulics.
Up and down like a roller coaster, I'm up inside ya.
I ain't quittin' till the show is over, 'cause I'm a rider.
In and out just like a robbery, I'll probably be a freak
And let you get on top of me, get her rockin' these
Nights full of Alize, a livin' legend.
You ain't heard about these niggaz play these Cali days.
Delores Tucker, youse a mother fucker.
Instead of tryin' to hep a nigga, you destroy a brother
Worse than the others. Bill Clinton, Mr. Bob Dole,
You're too old to understand the way the game is told.
You're lame, so I gotta hit you with the hot facts.
Want some on lease? I'm makin' millions, niggaz, top that.
They wanna censor me, they'd rather see me in a cell,
Livin' in hell. Only a few of us will live to tell.
Now everybody talkin' 'bout us. I could give a fuck.
I'd be the first one to bomb and cuss.
Nigga, tell me how you want it.
(To Chorus:)

Verse 3:
Raised as a youth, tell the truth, I got the scoop
On how to get a bulletproof, because I jumped from the roof
Before I was a teenager. Mobile phone, SkyPager,
Game rules, I'm livin' major. My adversaries
Is lookin' worried, they paranoid of gettin' buried.
One of us gon' see the cemetary.
My only hope to survive if I wish to stay alive,
Gettin' high, see the demons in my eyes before I die.
I wanna live my life and ball, make a couple million.
And then I'm chillin', fade 'em all.
These taxes got me crossed up and people tryin' to sue me.
Media is my business and they actin' like they know me.
Ha, ha, ha, but I'm a mash out, peel out.
I'm with it quick, I'se quick to whip that fuckin' steel out.
Yeah, nigga, it's some new shit, so better get up on it.
When ya see me, tell a nigga how you want it.
How do you want it?
(To Coda:)

I Ain't Mad At Cha

Written by TUPAC SHAKUR,
ETTERLENE JORDAN, DELMAR "DAZ" ARNAUD
and DANNY BOY STEWARD

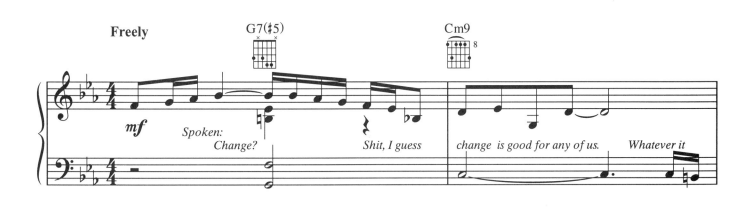

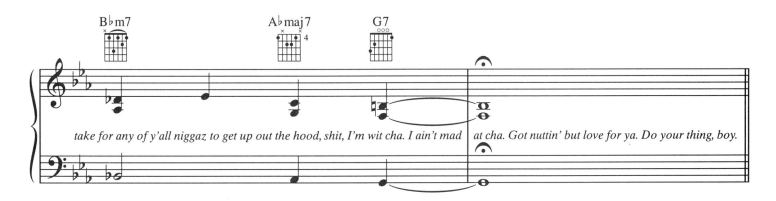

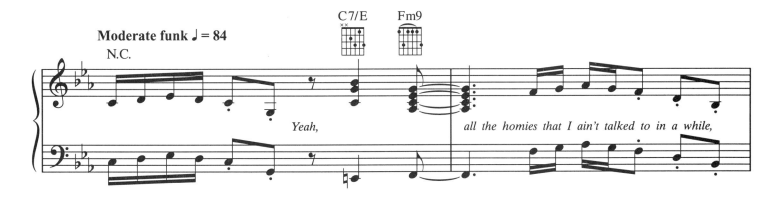

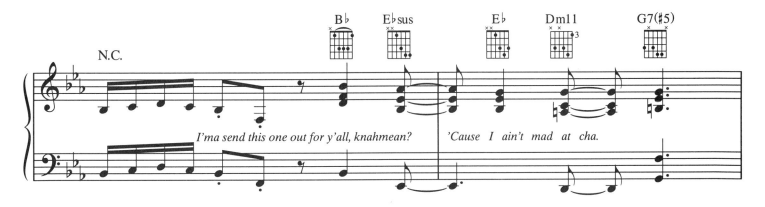

Verse 2:
We used to be like distant cousins, fightin', playin' dozens.
Whole nieghborhood buzzin', knowin' that we wasn't.
Used to catch us on the roof or behind the stairs.
I'm gettin' blitzed and I reminesce on all the times we shared.
Besides bumpin' 'n' grindin', wasn't nothin' on our mind.
In time we learned to live a life of crime.
Rewind us back to a time was much too young to know.
I caught a felony lovin' the way guns blow.
And even though we separated, you said that you'd wait.
Don't give nobody coochie while I be locked upstate.
I kiss my momma goodbye and wipe the tears from her lonely eyes.
Said, "I'll return, but I gotta fight, the fate's arrived."
Don't shed a tear 'cause momma, I ain't happy here.
I'm through trial, no more smiles for a couple years.
They got me goin' mad, I'm knockin' busters on they backs.
In my cell, thinkin', "Hell, I know one day I'll be back
As soon as I touch down."
I told my girl I'll be there, so prepare to get fucked down.
The homies wanna kick it, but I'm just laughin' at cha.
'Cause youse a down-ass bitch and I ain't mad at cha.
(To Chorus:)

Verse 3:
Well, guess who's movin' up, this nigga's ballin' now.
Bitches to be callin' to get it, hookers keep fallin' down.
He went from nuttin' to lots, ten carats to rock.
Went from a nobody nigga to the big man on the block.
He's Mister Local Celebrity, addicted to move a key.
Most hated by enemy, escape in the luxury.
See, first you was our nigga but you made it, so the choice is made.
Now we gotta slay you why you faded, in the younger days.
So full of pain while the weapons blaze.
Gettin' so high off that bomb, hopin' we make it to the better days.
'Cause crime pays, and in time, you'll find a rhyme'll blaze.
You'll feel the fire from the niggaz in my younger days.
So many changed on me, so many tried to plot.
That I keep a Glock beside me head, when will it stop?
Till God return me to my essence.
'Cause even as a adolescents, I refuse to be a convalescent.
So many questions, and they ask me if I'm still down.
I moved up out of the ghetto, so I ain't real now?
They got so much to say, but I'm just laughin' at cha.
You niggaz just don't know, but I ain't mad at cha.
(To Chorus:)

I Get Around

Written by TUPAC SHAKUR, GREGORY JACOBS,
RONALD BROOKS, SHIRLEY MURDOCK,
ROGER TROUTMAN and LARRY TROUTMAN

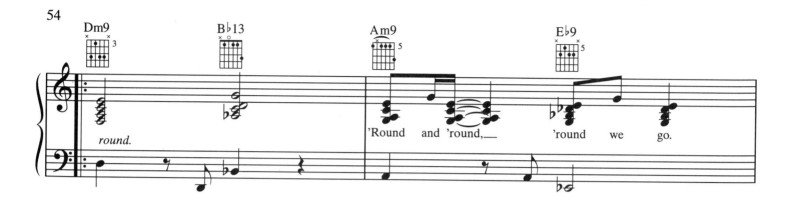

Repeat ad lib. and fade

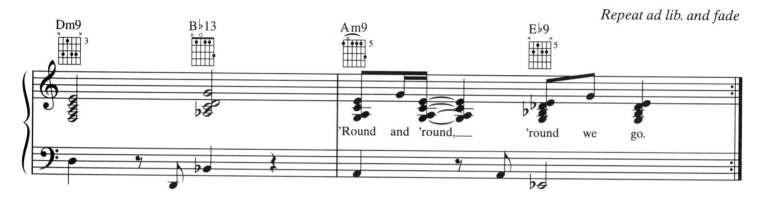

Verse 2:
Now you can tell from my everyday fits, I ain't rich.
So cease and desist with them tricks.
I'm just another black man caught up in the mix.
Tryin' to make a dollar out of fifteen cents.
Just 'cause I'm a freak, don't mean that we could hit the sheets.
Baby, I can see that you don't recognize me.
I'm Shock G, the one who put the satin on your panties.
Never knew a hooker who could share me.
I get around.
(To Bridge:)

Verse 3:
Fingertips on the hips as I tip, gotta get a tight grip.
Don't slip, loose lips sank ships.
It's a trip, I love it when she licks her lips, see me jockin'.
Put a little twist in her hips, 'cause I'm watchin'.
Conversations on the phone till the break of dawn.
Now we all alone, why the lights on?
Turn 'em off, time to set it off, get you wet and soft.
Somethin's on your mind, let it off.
(To Coda II)

I Wonder If Heaven Got A Ghetto

Written by TUPAC SHAKUR, LARRY GOODMAN,
DERRICK McDOWELL, ROGER TROUTMAN
and LARRY TROUTMAN

58

I wonder if Heaven got a ghetto.

Verse 2:
Here on Earth, tell me, what's black life worth?
A bottle of juice is no excuse, the truth hurts.
And even when you take the shit,
Move counties, get a lawyer, you can shake the shit.
Ask Rodney, LaTasha and many more.
It's been goin' on for years, there's plenty more.
When they ask me, "When will the violence cease?"
When your troops stop shootin' niggaz down in the street.
Niggaz had enough time to make a difference.
Bear witness, own our own business.
Word to God, 'cause it's hard tryin' to make ends meet.
First we couldn't afford shit, now everything's free.
So we loot, please don't shoot when you see me.
I'm takin' from them 'cause for years they would take it from me.
Now the tables have turned around.
You didn't listen until the niggaz burned it down.
And now Bush can't stop the hit,
Predicted the shit, in 2Pacalypse.
And for once, I was down with niggaz, felt good
In the hood, bein' around the niggaz, yeah.
And for the first time everybody let go.
And the streets is death row, I wonder if Heaven got a ghetto.
(To Chorus:)

Verse 3:
I see no changes, all I see is racist faces,
Misplaced hate makes disgrace to races.
We under, I wonder what it take to make this
One better place, let's erase the wait state.
Take the evil out the people, they'll be actin' right.
'Cause both black and white are smokin' crack tonight.
And only time we deal is when we kill each other.
It takes skill to be real, time to heal each other.
And though it seems heaven sent,
We ain't ready to have a black president, huh.
It ain't a secret, don't conceal the fact
The penetentiary's packed and it's filled with blacks.
I wake up in the morning and I ask myself,
"Is life worth living, should I blast myself?"
I'm tired of bein' poor, and even wosrse, I'm black.
My stomach hurts so, I'm lookin' for a purse to snatch.
Cops give a damn about a negro.
Pull a trigger, kill a nigga, he's a hero.
Mo' nigga, mo' nigga, mo' niggaz.
I'd rather be a dead than a po' nigga.
Let the Lord judge the criminals.
If I die, I wonder if Heaven got a ghetto.
(To Chorus:)

Chorus at ending:
Just think, if niggaz decide to retaliate
(Soldier in the house.)
I wonder if Heaven got a ghetto.

Me Against The World

Written by TUPAC SHAKUR, YAFEU FULA,
MALCOLM GREENIDGE, LEON WARE, MINNIE RIPERTON,
RICHARD RUDOLPH, BURT BACHARACH, HAL DAVID,
CARSTEN SCHACK and KENNETH KARLIN

% *Verse:*

N.C.

ecy? Stress in the city, the cops is hot for me. The *projects is full of bullets, the bodies is droppin'. There ain't no*

2.3. *See additional lyrics*

stoppin' me, constantly movin' while makin' millions, wit- *nessin' killings, leavin' dead bodies in abandoned buildings.*

Carries to children, 'cause they're illin'. Addicted to kill- *in' and the appeal from the cap peelin' without feelin'.*

But will they last or be blasted? Hardheaded bastard *Maybe he'll listen in his casket, the aftermath.*

B maj9 D+ D♭/E♭ E♭m7 E♭m7/A♭ A♭7sus

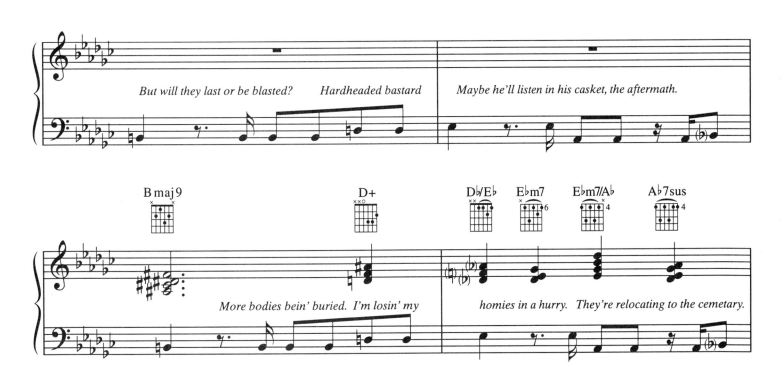

More bodies bein' buried. I'm losin' my *homies in a hurry. They're relocating to the cemetary.*

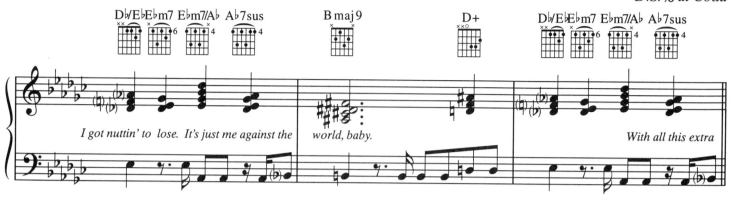

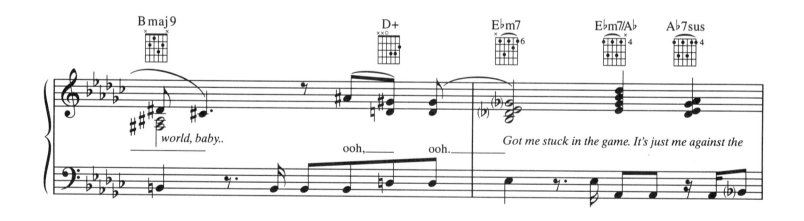

Repeat ad lib. and fade

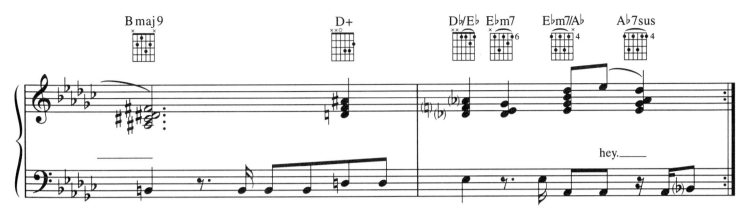

hey.____

Verse 2:
Could somebody help me?
I'm out here all by myself.
See ladies in stores, Baby Capone's, livin' wealthy.
Pictures of my birth on this earth is what I'm dreamin'.
Seein' Daddy's semen, full of crooked demons, already crazy
And screamin'. I guess them nightmares as a child
Had me scared, but left me prepared for a while.
Is there another route for a crooked outlaw?
Veteran, a villian, a young thug, who one day shall fall.
Everyday there's mo' death, and plus I'm doughless.
I'm seein' mo' reasons for me to proceed with thievin'.
Scheme on the scheming and leave they peeps grieving.
'Cause ain't no bucks to stack up, my nuts is backed up.
I'm about to act up, go load the Mac up, now watch me klacka.
Tried to make fat cuts, but yo, it ain't workin'.
And Evil's lurking, I can see him smirking.
When I got to go pervin', so what?
Go put some work in and make my mail, makin' sales.
Risking twenty-five with a 'L', but oh well.
(To Chorus:)

Verse 3:
With all this extra stressin',
The question I wonder is after death, after my last breath,
When will I finally get to rest? Through this supression
They punish the people that's askin' questions.
And those that possess, steal from the ones without posessions.
The message I stress: to make it stop, study your lessons.
Don't settle for less, even the genius askses questions.
Be grateful for blessings, don't ever change, keep your essence.
The power is in the people and politics we address.
Always do your best, don't let the pressure make you panic.
And when you get stranded, and things don't go the way you planned it,
Dreamin' of riches, in a position to make a difference.
Politicians and hypocrites, they don' wanna listen.
If I'm insane, it's the fame made a brother change.
It wasn't nuttin' like the game, it' just me against the world.
(To Chorus:)

Rap at Coda:
Heh, ha-ha-ha-ha-ha-ha, that's right.
I know it's hard sometimes, but uhh.
Remember one thing.
Through every dark night, there's a bright day after that.
So no matter how hard it get, stick your chest out.
Keep your head up and handle it.

Papa'z Song

Written by
TUPAC SHAKUR, JOE SAMPLE,
WILL JENNINGS and DEON EVANS

Funk shuffle ♩ = 86

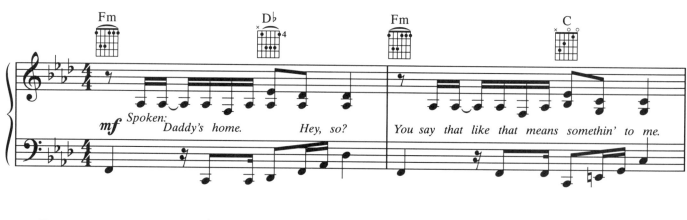

mf Spoken: Daddy's home. Hey, so? | You say that like that means somethin' to me.

You've been gone a mighty long mother fuckin' time | *for you to be comin' home talkin' that "Daddy's home" shit., (Nigga..)*

We been gettin' along fine just without you. | *Me, my brother and my mother.*

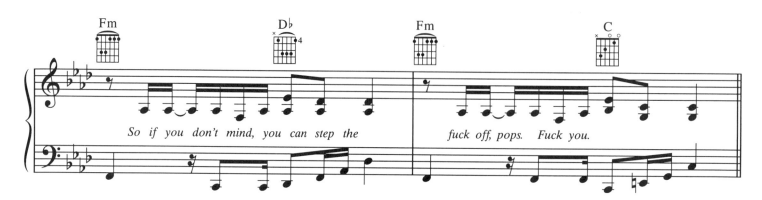

So if you don't mind, you can step the | *fuck off, pops. Fuck you.*

A different father every weekend. Be- fore we get to meet him, they break up before the week ends.

I'm gettin' sick of all the friendships As soon as we kick it he done split and the whole s**t ends quick.

How can I be a man if there's no role model? Strivin' to save my soul, I stay cold drinkin' a forty bottle. I'm so sorry. I'm so

Chorus:

sor - ry for all this time,_____ for all this
I'm so sorry.

time,_____ for all this time.__ I'm so sorry. I'm so

sor - ry for all this time,___ for all this time,___ for all this
I'm so sorry.

time.___ (So_ sor - ry, ba-by.) time.___ (So_ sor - ry, ba-by.)
I'm so

Verse 2:
Moms had to entertain many men.
Didn't wanna do it, but it's time to pay the rent again.
I'm gettin' a bit older and I'm startin' to be a bother.
Moms can't stand me 'cause I'm lookin' like my father.
Should I stay or run away? Tell me the answer.
Moms ignores me and avoids me like cancer.
Grow up rough and it's hard to understand stuff.
Moms was tough 'cause his poppa wasn't man enough.
Couldn't stand up to his own responsibilities.
Instead of takin' care of me, he'd rather live lavishly.
That's why I'll never be a father.
Unless you got the time, it's a crime, don't even bother.
That's when I started hatin' the phony smiles.
Said I was an only child.
Look at mama's lonely smile.
It's hard for a son to see his mother cry.
She only loves you but has to fuck with these other guys.
I'm so sorry.
(To Chorus:)

Verse 3:
Man child in the promised land couldn't afford many heroes.
Moms was the only one there, Pops was a no-show.
And oh, I guess ya didn't know that I would grow to be so strong.
Lookin' kinda pale, was it the ale. Oh, Pops was wrong.
Where was the money that you said you would send me.
Talked on the phone, you sounded so friendly.
Ask about school and my welfare.
But it's clear you ain't sincere. Hey, who the hell cares?
You think I'm blind but this time I see you comin', Jack.
You grabbed your coat, left us broke, now ain't no runnin' back.
Ask about my Moms like you loved her from the start.
Left her in the dark, she fell apart from a broken heart.
So don't even start with that "Wanna be your father" shit.
Don't even bother with your dollars, I don't need it.
I'll bury Moms like you left me all alone, G.
Now that I finally found you, Stay the fuck away from me.
I'm so sorry.
(To Chorus:)

Verse 4:
I never meant to leave but I was wanted.
Crossed too many people, every house I'd touch was haunted.
Had to watch the stangers, every brother was in danger.
If I was to keep you breathin', had to be out of range-a.
Had to move, one to lost my name and pick the number.
Made me watch my back, I had no happy home to run to.
Maybe it's my fault for bein' a father, livin' fast.
But livin' slow mean half the dough and you won't get no ass.
Hindsight shows me it was wrong all along.
I wanted to make some dough so you would grow to be so strong.
It took a little longer than I thought.
I slipped, got caught and sent to jail by the courts.
Now I'm doin' time and I wish you'd understand.
All I ever wanted was for you to be a man.
And grow to be the type you was meant to be.
Keep the war fightin' by the writings that you sent to me.
I'm so sorry.
(To Chorus:)

So Many Tears

Written by
TUPAC SHAKUR, ERIC VANDELL BAKER,
GREGORY JACOBS and STEVIE WONDER

Verse 2:
Now that I'm strugglin' in this business, by any means.
Label me greedy, gettin' green, but seldom seen.
And fuck the world, 'cause I'm cursed, I'm havin' visions
Of leavin' here in a hearse. God, can you feel me?
Take me away from all the pressure and all the pain.
Show me some happiness again, I'm goin' blind.
I spend my time in this cell, ain't livin' well.
I know my destiny is Hell, where did I fail?
My life is in denial and when I die,
Baptized in eternal fire, I'll shed so many tears.
(To Chorus:)

Verse 3:
Now I'm lost and I'm weary, so many tears.
I'm suicidal, so don't stand near me.
My every move is a calculated step to bring me closer
To embrace an early death. Now there's nothin' left.
There was no mercy on the streets, I couldn't rest.
I'm barely standin', 'bout to go to pieces, screamin' peace.
And though my soul was deleted, I couldn't see it.
I had my mind full of demons tryin' to break free.
They planted seeds and they hatched, sparkin' the flame
Inside my brain, like a match, such a dirty game.
No memories, just a misery.
Paintin' a picture of my enemies killin' me in my sleep.
Will I survive till the mornin', to see the sun?
Please, Lord, forgive me for all my sins, 'cause here I come.
Lord, I suffered through the years, (God) and shed so many tears.
(To Chorus:)

Verse 4:
Lord knows, I tried, been a witness to a homicide.
Seen drivebys takin' lives, little kids die.
Wonder why as I walk by.
Broken-hearted as I glance at the chalk line, gettin' high.
This ain't the life for me, I wanna change.
But ain't no future right for me, I'm stuck in the game.
I'm trapped inside a maze.
See this Tanqueray influenced me to gettin' crazy.
Disillusioned lately, I've been really wantin' babies,
So I could see a part of me that wasn't already shady.
Don't trust my lady, 'cause she's a part of this poison.
I'm hearin' noises, think she's fuckin' all my boys, can't take no more.
I'm fallin' to the floor, beggin' for the Lord to let me in.
To Heaven's door. Shed so many tears.
(Dear God, please let me in.)
(To Chorus:)

To Live & Die In L.A.

Written by
TUPAC SHAKUR, QUINCY DELIGHT JONES III
and VAL YOUNG

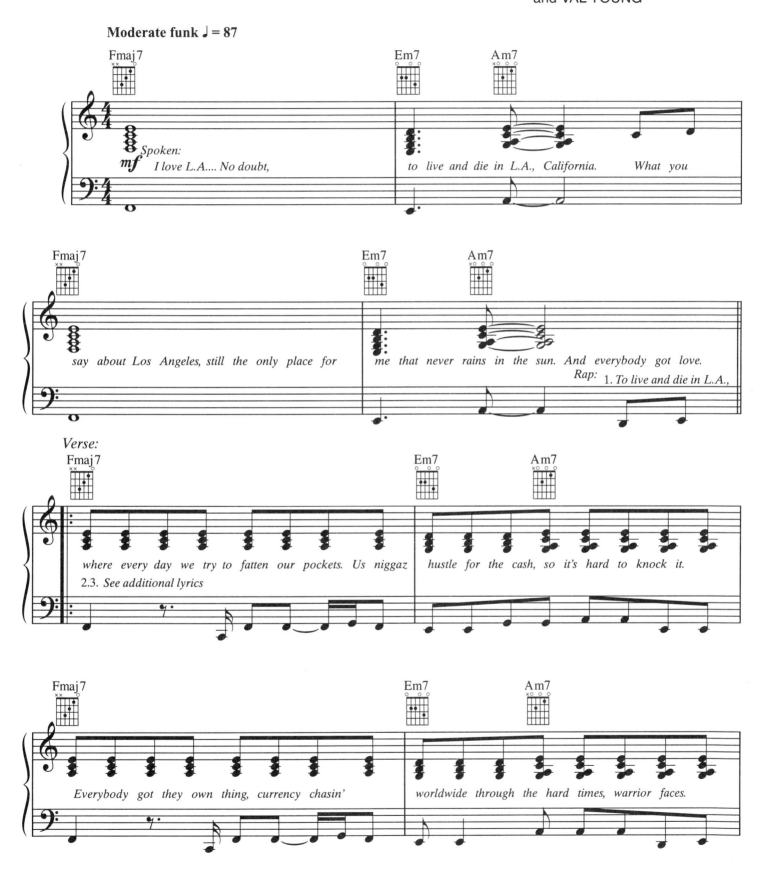

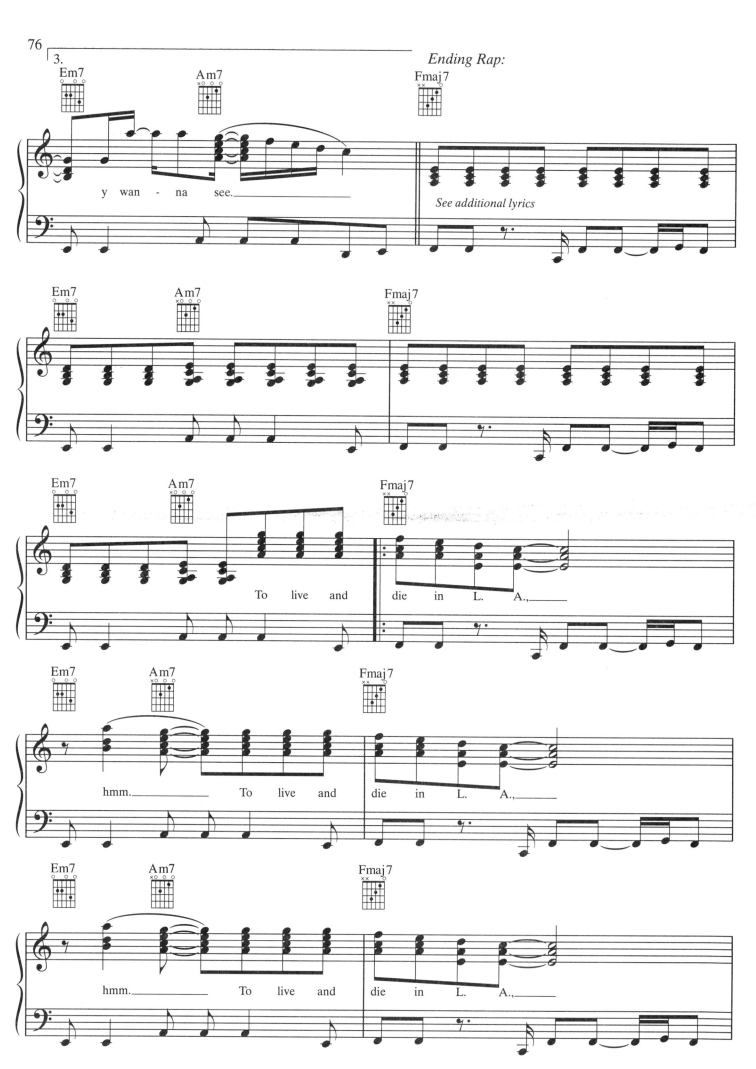

Verse 2:
It's the City of Angels and constant danger.
South Central L.A can't get no stranger.
Full of drama like a soap opera, on the curb.
Watchin' the ghetto bird helicopters, I observe.
So many niggaz gettin' three strikes, tossed in jail.
I swear the pen right across from hell. I can't cry
'Cause it's on now, I'm just a nigga on his own.
Livin' life thug style, so I can't smile.
Writin' to my peoples when they ask for pictures,
Thinkin' Cali just fun and bitches, ha,ha,ha.
Better learn about the dress code, B's and C's.
All them other nigga copycats, these is G's.
I love Cali like I love women,
'Cause every nigga in L.A. got a little bit of thug in him.
We might fight amongst each other, but I promise you this.
We'll burn the bitch down, get us pissed.
To live and die in L.A. Let my O.G. sing.
(To Chorus:)

Verse 3:
It wouldn't be L.A. without Mexicans?
Black love, brown pride and the sets again.
Pete Wilson tryin' to see us all broke, I'm on some bullshit.
Out for everything they owe, remember K-Day,
Weekends, Crenshaw, M.L.K.
Automatics rang free, niggaz lost they way.
Gang signs bein' showed, nigga love your hood.
But recognize and it's all good. Where the weed at?
Niggaz gettin' shermed out.
Snoop Dogg in this muhfucka permed out, M.O.B.
Big Suge in the Low-Low, bounce and turn.
Dogg Pound in the Lex, wit an ounce to burn.
Got them Watts niggaz with me, O.F.T.B.
They got some hash, took the stash, left the rest for me.
Neckbone, Tre, Head Ron, Bunchy, too.
Big Rock got knocked, but this one's for you.
I hit the studio and drop a jewel, hopin' it pay.
Gettin' high, watchin' time fly, to live and die in L.A.
Let my angels sing.
(To Chorus:)

Ending Rap:
This go out for 92.3 and 106.
All the radio stations that be bumpin' my shit.
Makin' my shit sells katruple, quitraple platinum, he, he.
This go out to all the magazines that support a nigga,
All the real mother fuckers,
All the stores, the mom and pop spots,
A&R people, all y'all mother fuckers.
L.A., California Love, part mother fucker, two.
Without gay ass Dre.

2 Of Americaz Most Wanted

Written by
TUPAC SHAKUR, DELMAR "DAZ" ARNAUD
and SNOOP DOGGY DOG

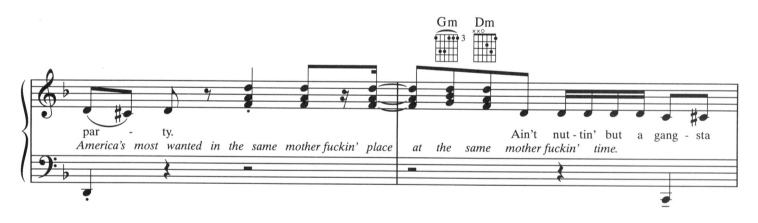

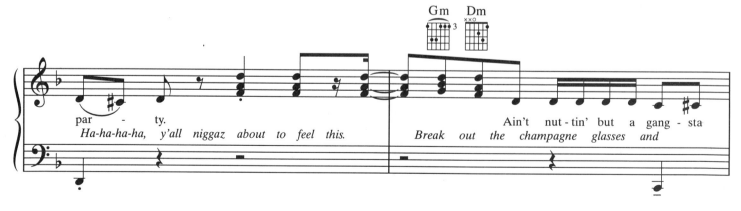

80

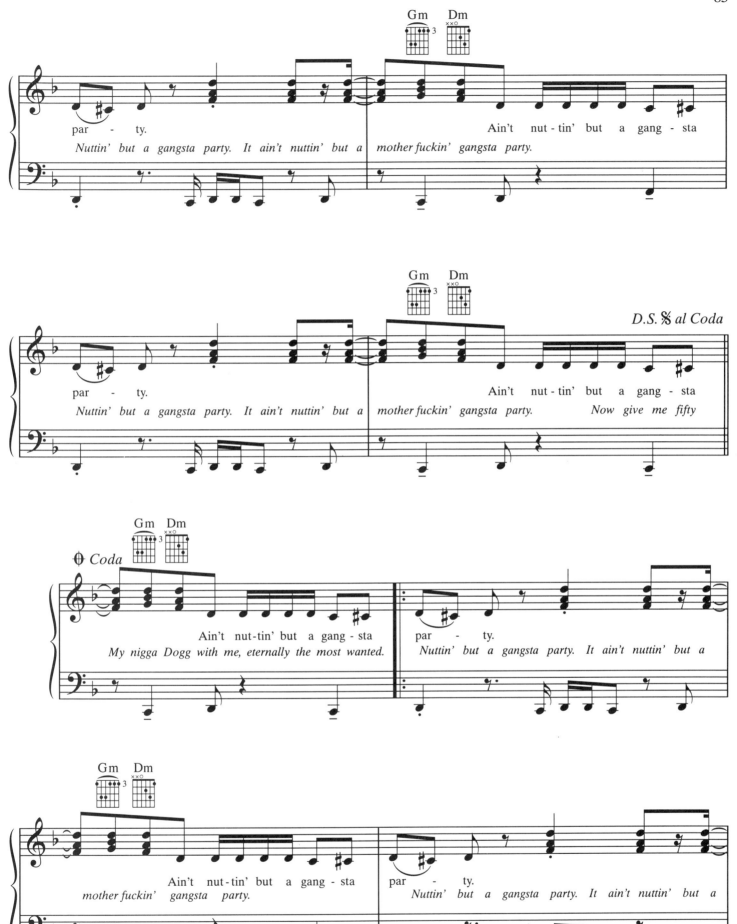

Repeat ad lib. and fade

mother fuckin' gangsta party.   Ain't   nut - tin'   but   a   gang - sta

Verse 2:
Now give me fifty feet.
Defeat is not my destiny, release me to the streets
And keep what ever's left of me.
Jealousy is misery, suffering is grief.
Better be prepared when you cowards fuck wit me.
I bust and flee, these niggaz must be crazy, what?
There ain't no mercy mother fuckers who can fade the thugs.
(Ha-ha-ha-ha, right.)
You thought it was, but it wasn't, now disappear.
Bow down in the presence of a boss player.
It's like, cuz blood, gangbangin',
Everybody in the party doin' dope, slangin'.
You got to have papers in this world.
You might get your first snatch before your eyes swerl.
Ya doin' your job, everyday.
And then you work so hard till ya hair turn gray.
Let me tell you about life, and 'bout the way it is.
You see we live by the gun, so we die by the gun's kids.
They tell me not to roll with my Glock,
So now I gotta throw it away.
Floatin' in the black Benz, tryin' to do a show a day.
They wonder how I live, with five shots.
Niggaz is hard to kill on my block.
Schemes for currency and doe related.
Affiliated with the hustlers, so we made it.
No answers to questions, I'm tryin' to get up on it.
My nigga Dogg with me, eternally the most wanted.
(To Coda)

Final Fade:
Bitch, where ya at?
Death row...